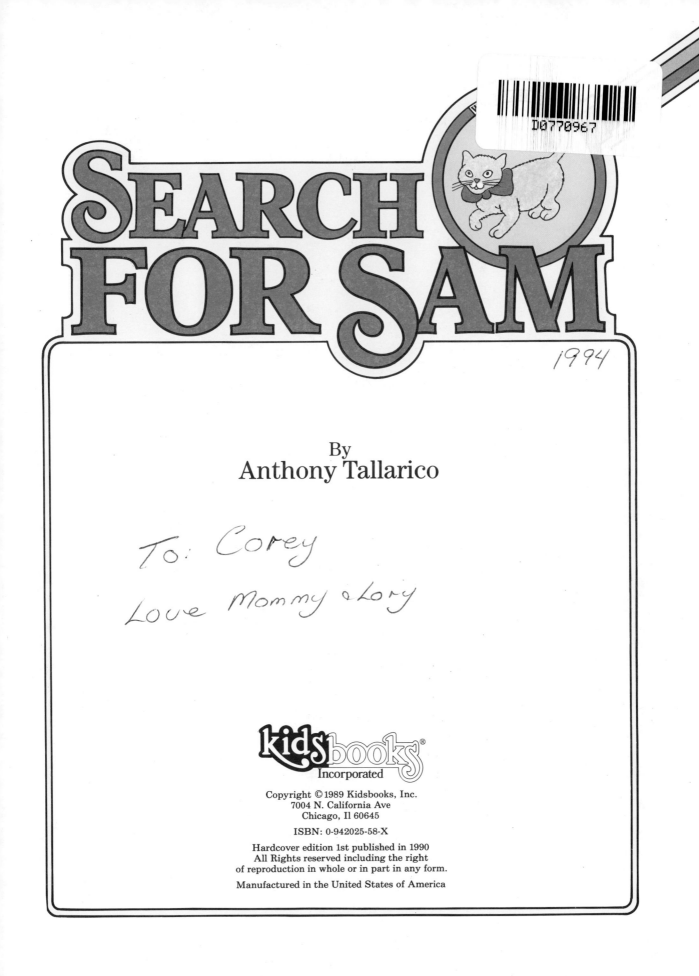

SEARCH FOR SAM

1994

By
Anthony Tallarico

To: Corey

Love Mommy & Lory

kidsbooks ®
Incorporated

Copyright © 1989 Kidsbooks, Inc.
7004 N. California Ave
Chicago, Il 60645

ISBN: 0-942025-58-X

Hardcover edition 1st published in 1990

SEARCH FOR SAM IN CAT CITY AND . . .

- ☐ 2 Balloons
- ☐ Broken window
- ☐ Bus stop
- ☐ Car on sidewalk
- ☐ Catmobile
- ☐ Cat plane
- ☐ Clock
- ☐ Clown cat
- ☐ Cyclist
- ☐ "Do Not Litter"
- ☐ 2 Dogs
- ☐ Flat tire
- ☐ Flower pot
- ☐ Garbage truck
- ☐ 3 Ghost cats
- ☐ Human
- ☐ Ice skater
- ☐ Kite
- ☐ Kitty and Kats Avenues
- ☐ Locomotive
- ☐ 3 Mice
- ☐ Movie theater
- ☐ Penguin
- ☐ Piano
- ☐ Policecat
- ☐ Radio
- ☐ Roller skater
- ☐ Santa Claus
- ☐ Scarf
- ☐ 3 Sharks
- ☐ Ship on wheels
- ☐ 2 Skateboards
- ☐ Sleeping cat
- ☐ Sleigh
- ☐ Sock
- ☐ 5 Traffic accidents
- ☐ 8 Trash cans
- ☐ Waiter
- ☐ "What Time Is It?"
- ☐ Wind-up car

SEARCH FOR SAM
ON FRIDAY THE
13TH AND . . .

- ☐ Apple
- ☐ Ax
- ☐ Balloon
- ☐ 7 Bats
- ☐ 4 Black cats
- ☐ Bomb
- ☐ Candy cane
- ☐ Chicken
- ☐ Coffin
- ☐ Condos
- ☐ Cow
- ☐ Football
- ☐ "Ghost Office"
- ☐ 6 Ghosts
- ☐ Heart
- ☐ "Helping Hand"
- ☐ Junior vampire
- ☐ Kite eater
- ☐ Mad doctor
- ☐ Mailbox
- ☐ Man's head
- ☐ Mirror
- ☐ Mouse
- ☐ "No Screaming"
- ☐ Paint bucket
- ☐ Pirate
- ☐ 13 Pumpkins
- ☐ Quicksand
- ☐ Rabbit
- ☐ Ship
- ☐ Shovel
- ☐ Skull
- ☐ Snake
- ☐ 13 "13s"
- ☐ Trunk
- ☐ Turtle
- ☐ TV set
- ☐ Two-headed
  monster
- ☐ Vampire

SEARCH FOR SAM AT THE FAT CAT HEALTH CLUB AND . . .

SEARCH FOR SAM ON VACATION AND . . .

- ☐ Arrow
- ☐ Balloon
- ☐ Barbecue
- ☐ Barrel
- ☐ Bicycle
- ☐ Bull
- ☐ Dog
- ☐ Downhill skier
- ☐ 3 Ducks
- ☐ "Fast Cat"
- ☐ "Hi Mom!"
- ☐ Hobby horse
- ☐ Hot dog
- ☐ Igloo
- ☐ Jump rope
- ☐ Lighthouse
- ☐ Lion
- ☐ Motorcyclist
- ☐ Net
- ☐ Octopus
- ☐ Radio
- ☐ "S.S. Meow"
- ☐ 2 Sailboats
- ☐ Sand castle
- ☐ Scuba diver
- ☐ Shark
- ☐ Shovel
- ☐ Skateboard
- ☐ Sludge
- ☐ Starfish
- ☐ Sunflower
- ☐ Surfer
- ☐ Super cat
- ☐ Swordfish
- ☐ Telescope
- ☐ Tennis racket
- ☐ 3 Turtles
- ☐ 3 Umbrellas
- ☐ Uphill skier

SEARCH FOR SAM
AT THE MIDNIGHT
MEOWING AND . . .

- ☐ Alarm clock
- ☐ 3 "Arf"
- ☐ 2 Birds
- ☐ Broken window
- ☐ 3 Brooms
- ☐ 7 Cannonballs
- ☐ "Cat Power!"
- ☐ Dog
- ☐ 2 Dog bones
- ☐ Dog dish
- ☐ Doll
- ☐ Egg
- ☐ 2 Fish bones
- ☐ Floor mat
- ☐ 3 Flower pots
- ☐ Ghost
- ☐ Hockey stick
- ☐ "Hush"
- ☐ "I like it!"
- ☐ Loudest
    screamer
- ☐ Microphone
- ☐ Mouse
- ☐ "No Meowing
    Zone"
- ☐ Open gate
- ☐ Phonograph
- ☐ Piggy bank
- ☐ Pillow
- ☐ Pumpkin
- ☐ Rhino
- ☐ Shoe
- ☐ Sleeping cat
- ☐ Slice of pizza
- ☐ Spaceship
- ☐ Stool
- ☐ Tin can
- ☐ Tire
- ☐ 4 Trash cans
- ☐ Witch
- ☐ Yo-yo

SEARCH FOR SAM AT THE DISCO AND . . .

- ☐ Ballerina
- ☐ 7 Balloons
- ☐ Break dancer
- ☐ Clown
- ☐ Cook
- ☐ Cowboy
- ☐ Dark glasses
- ☐ Disco duck
- ☐ Disco pig
- ☐ Dizzy cat
- ☐ Doctor
- ☐ Dog
- ☐ Duck
- ☐ Ear plugs
- ☐ Earrings
- ☐ Flower pot
- ☐ Hard hat
- ☐ Horn player
- ☐ Indian
- ☐ Karate cat
- ☐ Lamp shade
- ☐ 2 Mice
- ☐ Pig
- ☐ Pirate
- ☐ Pizza
- ☐ Police cat
- ☐ Rabbit
- ☐ Record eater
- ☐ Records
- ☐ 2 Rhinos
- ☐ Roller skates
- ☐ Scarf
- ☐ Skier
- ☐ Sleeping cat
- ☐ Snow cat
- ☐ 10 Speakers
- ☐ Swinging globe
- ☐ Top hat
- ☐ Record

SEARCH FOR SAM AT THE BATTLE OF CATS AND MICE AND . . .

SEARCH FOR SAM IN ANCIENT EGYPT AND . . .

SEARCH FOR SAM
AT THE CAT SHOW
AND . . .

- ☐ Banjo
- ☐ Beach chair
- ☐ Bird
- ☐ Black cat
- ☐ Cat costume
- ☐ Cat guard
- ☐ Cat in a hat
- ☐ Cat on a
  woman's head
- ☐ Clown
- ☐ Cow
- ☐ Curtain
- ☐ 2 Dogs
- ☐ Elephant
- ☐ Fat cat
- ☐ 2 Fish bowls
- ☐ Fishing pole
- ☐ Groucho cat
- ☐ Hobo cat
- ☐ Jogging cat
- ☐ 3 Judges
- ☐ Light bulb
- ☐ Lion
- ☐ "Moo Juice"
- ☐ Mouse
- ☐ Photographer
- ☐ Pizza
- ☐ Pool
- ☐ "Princess"
- ☐ Scaredy cat
- ☐ Scarf
- ☐ Scratching
  post
- ☐ Sombrero
- ☐ Sunglasses
- ☐ Telescope
- ☐ "The Real
  1st Prize"
- ☐ Tombstone
- ☐ Trombone
- ☐ "Wanted" poster
- ☐ Witch

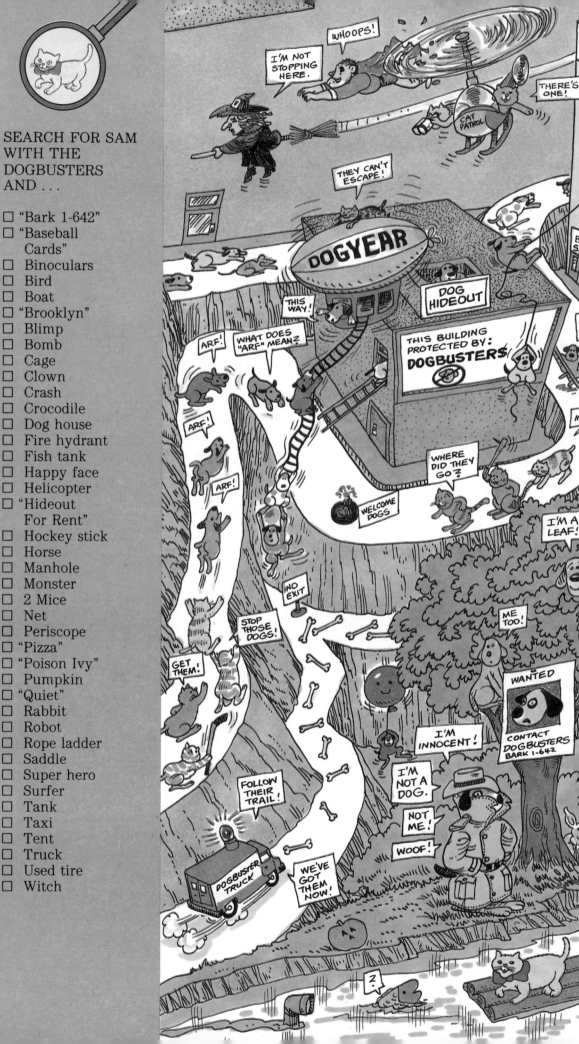

SEARCH FOR SAM AT THE NORTH POLE AND . . .

SEARCH FOR SAM   FIND FREDDIE   HUNT FOR HECTOR   LOOK FOR LISA